Simon Dunning
August 2006

ARGYLL & SUTHERLAND HIGHLANDERS

ARGYLL & SUTHERLAND HIGHLANDERS

ALASTAIR CAMPBELL OF AIRDS

TEMPUS

Frontispiece: The Argyll & Sutherland Highlanders were delighted by the appointment in 1947 of the then HRH Princess Elizabeth as their Colonel-in-Chief, one of the first regiments to be so honoured. For over half a century, Her Majesty has held this position and throughout that time has never failed in her interest and support for the regiment. This picture shows her at Stirling Castle for the centenary celebrations for the Battle of Balaklava at which the 93rd Highlanders formed The Thin Red Line. With her is the Colonel of the regiment, General Sir Gordon MacMillan of MacMillan and Knap and behind, two archers of The Queen's Body Guard for Scotland, left, Lt-Col. I E.P. Buchanan and Brigadier Hector Greenfield.

First published 2005

Tempus Publishing Limited
The Mill, Brimscombe Port,
Stroud, Gloucestershire, GL5 2QG
www.tempus-publishing.com

British Library Cataloguing in Publication Data.
A catalogue record for this book is available from the British Library.

ISBN 0 7524 3538 8

Typesetting and origination by Tempus Publishing Limited.
Printed in Great Britain.

Contents

Sgt-Maj. Donald Murray together with a Corporal and a bandboy of the 93rd Sutherland Highlanders taken in the year of the Mutiny, 1857, showing several articles of uniform still in wear today. The band at this period were clothed in white tunics with red collar and cuffs.

Introduction and Acknowledgements

This is a collection of photographs relating to the Argyll & Sutherland Highlanders, culled from the regimental archives in Stirling Castle and covering the period from 1881, when the 91st and 93rd Highlanders were amalgamated, to the present day, that is to say, roughly, the second half of the life of the regiment. The period is a momentous one, including as it does the apogee of Empire, two World Wars, the Cold War, the relinquishing of the Empire and a new role as world peace-keepers and guards against world terrorism.

The photographs are in approximate chronological sequence but the emphasis throughout has been on including good and interesting photographs rather than producing a balanced history. Thus the sections on the two World Wars are relatively limited and depend largely on the Imperial War Museum, whose help is acknowledged with gratitude; we seem, as a regiment, to have been all too meticulous in observing the official ban on the use of private cameras in wartime. And the last period of thirty-plus years, during which the 1st Battalion has put in so much dogged and devoted service in Northern Ireland, does not easily lend itself to exciting photography even if, all too often, it has provided more than enough excitement for those taking part. So, there will be events which do not figure in what follows, simply because there are no good photographs available.

But, having said this, the collection is one which is full of interest and variety, as befits a regiment whose record of service to the Crown is unsurpassed. One aspect which the photographs bring out is the sense of identity which a great regiment possesses and which the technocrats meddle with at risk; it is compounded of a strong sense of place; a continuing link and identification with the area of Scotland from which the regiment draws the vast majority of its members and a link with the past cemented by the number of members of the same family who have soldiered with the regiment generation after generation, and who continue to do so today.

It was in 1794 that the Duke of Argyll deputed his kinsman, Campbell of Lochnell, to raise a Regiment of Argyllshire Highlanders. Initially numbered the 98th, it was soon after renumbered the 91st. It saw early service at the Cape, in the Peninsular War, in reserve at Waterloo and on several occasions in South Africa. In 1809, the 91st, in company with some other Highland Corps, lost the Highland dress, tartan trews eventually being adopted in 1864 when the regiment's Highland identity was restored. In 1881 the Cardwell Reforms twinned the 91st with the 93rd, raised by Maj. General William Wemyss in 1800. After early service at the Cape of Good Hope, the 93rd came into prominence in the Crimean War where it formed the Thin Red Line at Balaklava in the Crimea before further distinguishing itself in the Indian Mutiny, notably at the Relief of Lucknow where the regiment won no less than six VCs.

These two very different units were brought together to form today's Argyll & Sutherland Highlanders. Each of the two Regular battalions continued to keep a lively memory of their respective identities as the 91st and the 93rd. The new regiment was given an area comprising the counties of Argyll and Bute, Stirlingshire, Clackmannan, Renfrew and Dumbarton with the infantry Militia and Volunteer Corps contained therein, who then became part of the regiment.

Regulars, Militia and Volunteers all saw service in the Boer War of 1899-1902 as they did in the dreadful War of 1914 -18 in which twenty-seven battalions of the regiment served, including those Service Battalions raised especially for the conflict. The Argylls sustained no less than 431 officers and 6,475 Other Ranks killed with many thousands more wounded. The regiment saw service in Egypt, Palestine, Gallipoli, Macedonia, Italy and above all, in France and Flanders on the Western Front.

In the Second World War, fewer Battalions took part but the regiment distinguished itself in North Africa, Eritrea, Abyssinia, the Sudan, Crete, Malaya and Singapore, and north-west Europe. Overall, the Argyll & Sutherland Highlanders won seventy-eight Battle Honours in the First World War and sixty in the Second World War.

The coming of so-called peace brought little respite for the Argylls. The 1st Battalion, now the only Regular one after amalgamation with the 2nd Battalion in 1947, saw action in Palestine before taking part in the particularly nasty war of 1950–52 in Korea where Maj. Muir won the regiment's last Victoria Cross. They took part in the Suez operation in 1956, were on active service in Cyprus in 1958–59, served three tours in Borneo during the confrontation with Indonesia in the late 1960s and were among the last troops out of Aden in 1969 after their famous retaking of Crater. The same year they found themselves on active service once more, this time in Northern Ireland. At this time they were the most operationally experienced Battalion in the post-war British Army.

It was Northern Ireland which was to dominate their record for the next thirty-five years – years of hard, monotonous and always dangerous soldiering in which constant alertness and aggression when required have been combined with patient restraint and building the confidence of the strife-ridden community of Ulster. The same qualities have been displayed with the Argylls' recent deployment to Iraq, and now to Bosnia. Throughout this period the Battalion alternated active service tours in Ulster with home stations in the UK and Germany, together with postings to such places as Hong Kong, the Falkland Islands, Cyprus and training tours to locations as far apart as Kenya and Canada.

My grateful thanks to my namesake Maj. Alastair Campbell, the current Regimental Secretary, to Rod Mackenzie, indefatigable Assistant Curator of the Regimental Museum and to Hamish Gauld; their help has been invaluable. I must also thank Lt-Col. Alastair Scott-Elliott, a former Commanding Officer of the 1st Battalion and Regimental Secretary, and Mrs Gail Scott-Elliott; the former for much advice and practical assistance and the latter for much kindness and hospitality. My thanks also to the editors with Tempus Publishing, Nicola Sweet, and Campbell McCutcheon, whose late father Bob, a good friend, started to undertake the task of compiling this book which was cut short almost immediately by his untimely death. And finally to my son Jamie for assistance with the mysteries of the computer.

The future of the regiment is unsettled as I write, with its inclusion in the new Royal Regiment of Scotland. As in 1881, a proud individual tradition is less than happy with possible dilution in a larger entity. One thing, however, is sure – the men of the Argylls, in whatever guise, will continue to soldier on, facing whatever comes their way with courage, invincible cheerfulness and determination, and mindful of their great heritage; for them as for the long lines of those who have gone before, once an Argyll, always an Argyll.

Alastair Campbell of Airds
Unicorn Pursuivant of Arms
Inverawe
May 2005

one

The forerunners 1794–1881

When, in 1871, HRH Princess Louise, Queen Victoria's fourth daughter, married the Marquess of Lorne, heir to the Duke of Argyll, Chief of Clan Campbell, the 91st furnished a Guard of Honour for their wedding in the Chapel Royal, Windsor Castle. When the new regiment was formed in 1881 it was initially given the title of Princess Louise's (Sutherland & Argyll Highlanders). This was almost immediately changed to Princess Louise's (Argyll & Sutherland Highlanders). It only adopted its present title in 1920. Until her death in 1939, Princess Louise always very much regarded the regiment as hers; officially appointed Colonel-in-Chief in 1914, she visited the various Battalions regularly and took a constant interest in their doings.

In May–June 1872, the 91st found the Royal Guard for Queen Victoria's visit to Balmoral. At this time the Lowland regiments were still clad in ordinary Line uniform and tartan trews were only worn by certain Highland regiments, among whom were the 91st, who had reassumed tartan of Campbell of Cawdor pattern in 1864.

The 91st drawn up on the Esplanade, Edinburgh Castle, in 1874. The Pioneer Section are in front, followed by the Pipes and Drums and the Military Band. The Field Officers are mounted and the Battalion is made up of eight companies. The pipers are wearing feather bonnets.

Officers of the 91st on active service in Zululand, 1879. Still in scarlet but shaving now optional and some of the helmets are khaki. The regiment's main engagement was at Ginginhlovu – known to the Jocks as 'Gin Gin I love you' – where, on 2 April 1879, they fought off the main Zulu attack on the British square.

Active service in Zululand, 1879; the firing line is wreathed in smoke, answered by enemy fire from further up the hill. A company in reserve watches the action. Taking cover was still an unknown art; indeed, officers were expected to walk up and down the firing line, ignoring enemy bullets, in order to 'steady' the men.

Sergeants of the 91st shortly before amalgamation with the 93rd. Trews and plaids of Campbell of Cawdor tartan – the Government sett with the addition of a red and a light blue line – had been worn since tartan had been restored to the regiment in 1864; strange as it seems, no one apparently could remember that the original tartan of the regiment had been the plain Government sett.

A group of NCOs and men of the 93rd, *c.*1860. The uniform was largely adopted by the new regiment and several articles seen here are still being worn. Note the Sergeant in the centre wearing an early form of mess-dress, his shell jacket worn open with the lapels turned back. His companions to right and left are even more relaxed, in white duck trousers and some form of blazer with rank badges attached.

Officers of the 93rd in India prior to the outbreak of the Mutiny. The new regiment was to adopt, in essence, the uniform of the kilted 93rd and most of the items here seen are still worn today.

Officers of the new 1st Battalion have adopted most of the new regimental uniform but for the moment retain their 91st pattern glengarries and badges.

The new regiment now also contained a number of Volunteer units – the forerunners of today's Territorials. Each had its own uniform, which was gradually changed to that of the parent regiment. Here are two officers of the Renfrewshire Rifle Volunteers, the one on the right a member of the Greenock Highland Company.

A grand old Highlander. The Sergeant-Major (RSM) of the 93rd, *c.*1870. Sgt-Maj. Motion joined the 93rd in 1849; he transferred to the Stirling Militia as Sgt-Maj. in 1870 and served for a further fourteen years by which time it had become the 3rd Militia Battalion of the Regiment.

Princess Louise, from whom the regiment took its title, was the fourth daughter of Queen Victoria. In 1871, she married the Marquess of Lorne, future 9th Duke of Argyll. Her pipe banner displays the arms of her husband with a Marquess's coronet and her own with the coronet of a Royal Princess. Overall is the boar's head crest of the Duke of Argyll, Chief of Clan Campbell.

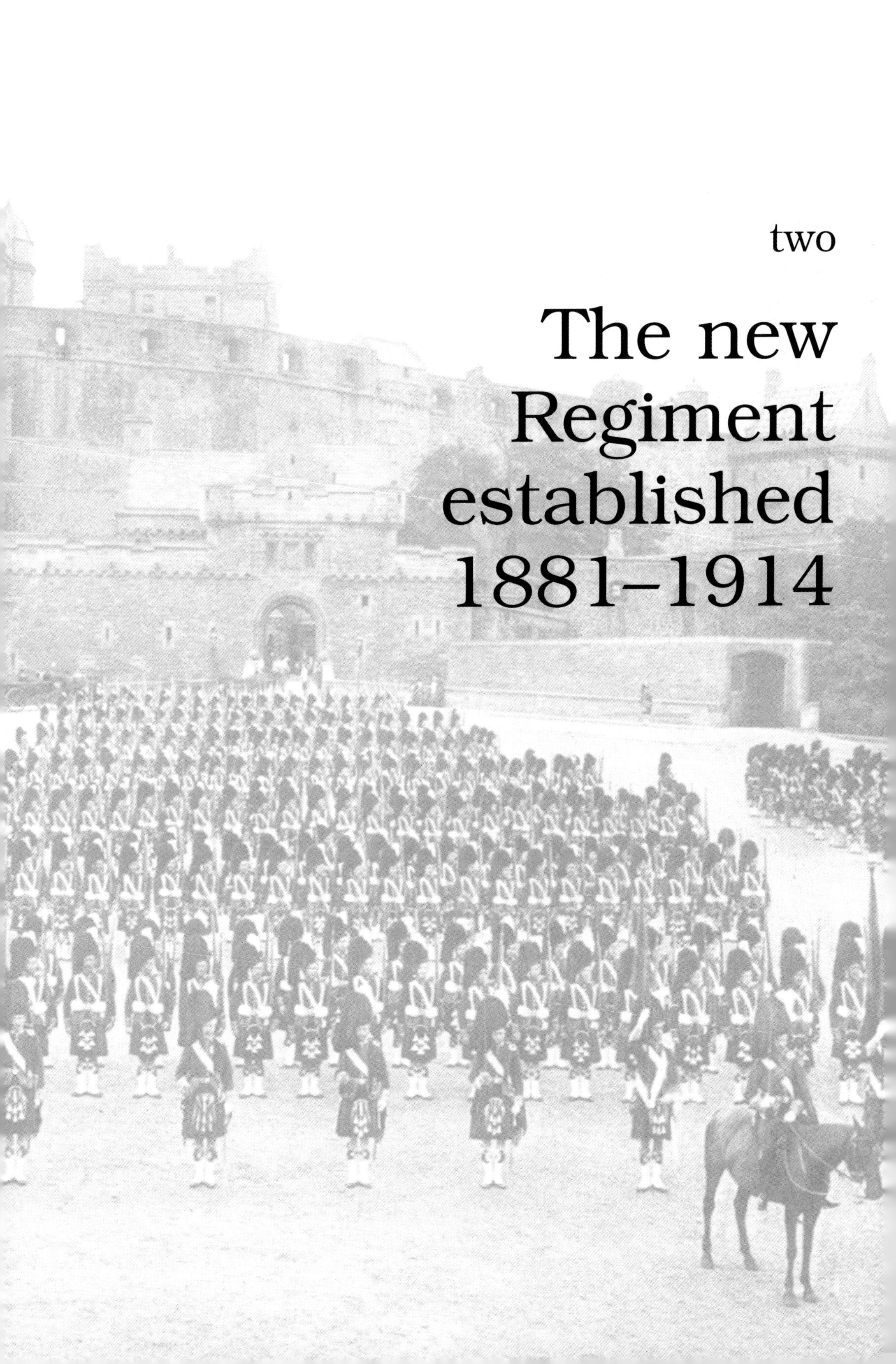

two

The new Regiment established 1881–1914

Changing of the Guard at Hyde Park Barracks, May 1885; the 93rd take over from the Black Watch.

The 1st Battalion on parade at bayonet practice, Colombo, *c.*1887. They have clearly been instructed to watch the birdie instead of keeping their eyes to the front!

A 1st Battalion Guard mounted on the wine chais or warehouses, Capetown, South Africa, *c.*1885 – no doubt a precaution against pilfering. The distinctive shape of Table Mountain is outlined at left.

The 93rd mount the Prison Guard at Mean Mir, India, in 1895. Scarlet and tartan have been discarded in the hot weather season for all-white tropical uniform and the Guard have been spared the march to the prison by a more relaxing form of transport.

The 3rd (Militia) Battalion practise forming square during their annual month's training at Cambusbarron Camp, Stirling, with the Highland hills in the background, *c.*1881. Forming square to repel cavalry or native hordes was still the standard infantry tactic.

In 1897 the 93rd were called on to join the Tochi Valley Expedition on India's North-West Frontier, against the Wazirs who had killed a number of British officers. Although not engaged in any fighting, the Battalion lost several men through heatstroke, the daytime temperature in the shade reaching nearly 120 degrees.

In 1898 the 91st sent the Pipes and Drums, the Band and a detachment on a recruiting march in Argyll. The weather is as usual, there is not a recruit in sight and yet the party looks cheerful enough as it descends the Pass of Melfort.

Maxim Gun section of the 5th Volunteer Battalion, forerunners of the famous 8th (Argyllshire) Battalion. Brought into the regimental family by the 1881 Cardwell reforms, the unit is still wearing items of its old uniform combined with that of the Argyll & Sutherland Highlanders. Note the Campbell boar's head on the sporran and the diced balmoral, reminiscent of the headgear worn in the 1950s and 1960s. The kilt is still the old pattern Campbell of Cawdor previously worn by the Argyllshire Rifle Volunteers.

Officers of the 5th Volunteer Battalion, 1889. The towering bearded figure is that of the CO, Lt-Col. John Wingfield, Malcolm of Poltalloch (later Lord Malcolm of Poltalloch CB VD), whose family have produced several generations of officers for the regiment. Some articles of dress of the old Argyll Highland Rifles were still being worn.

A contrast from the same scene almost twenty years previously; the 91st are now resplendent in full kilted Highland dress; the formation is much the same only the Pioneers and both bands are now on the left flank of the Battalion. The CO is mounted in front, with his accompanying Bugler.

The Battalion tailors' shop, as always hard at work. An essential part of the Battalion's appearance was the fitting of uniforms. Until recent times, the Battalion also had its own kilt-makers. The dog may or may not be stuffed!

Above: The 3rd (Militia) Battalion Cycling Club, *c.*1881. Note the variety of dress, including a form of mixed dress not usually seen: tunic open, civilian shirt and tie, glengarry and trousers tucked into stockings. Cycling at the time was what today would be known as cool!

Left: One of our most distinguished Argylls, now largely forgotten. Lt-Gen. Sir David Henderson KCB KCVO DSO was commissioned into the regiment in 1883. He won his DSO in the Boer War as Lord Kitchener's Director of Intelligence. He was appointed Director-General of Military Aeronautics in 1913 and GOC The Royal Flying Corps 1914–1917. Even Lord Trenchard, who is referred to as the 'Father of the Royal Air Force' stated that the title belonged by rights to Sir David.

Lord Roberts visited the 1st Battalion in Dublin in October 1899 before they left for South Africa; on his right the CO, Lt-Col. G.L.J. Goff, who was to be killed in the forthcoming war; second from left, Lt Gervase Thorpe, later a General and Colonel of the Regiment; fourth from left, Maj. A. Wilson, also later a General and sixth from left in the rear rank, 2nd-Lt W.G. Neilson, whose son and grandson served with distinction in the regiment.

The 91st arrived at Cape Town on 17 November 1899 and set off to join the Highland Brigade. The sporran set against a dark kilt made an excellent aiming mark for Boer marksmen; it was soon replaced by a khaki kilt-apron and khaki blanco was substituted for the white used on the equipment shown in this photo. At this stage the British Army had little notion of what was facing them; they were to learn fieldcraft the hard way in the months ahead.

On 11 December 1899 the Highland Brigade carried out a dawn attack against the Boer position at Magersfontein Hill. This involved a night approach across the scrubby plain, which was carried out with some difficulty. Unfortunately, the Boer position was in trenches at the foot of the hill, not on top of it as had been thought; the Highlanders were taken by surprise at short range in the open and pinned down under a murderous fire which inflicted serious casualties.

There was initial panic and confusion, which could have turned the confrontation into a rout. It was stopped by Cpl Jimmy MacKay of the Argylls who stood up, facing the hail of bullets, and played 'The Campbells are Coming' to steady his comrades, an act which might well have merited a Victoria Cross. His example was followed by pipers of the other regiments and the Brigade held on although a number of sporadic attempts to rush the enemy proved costly and fruitless; eventually, that afternoon, the order was given to retire. Among the slain were Brigadier-General Wauchope, the Brigade Commander and the Argylls' CO, Lt-Col. Lionel Goff. It was a serious defeat for the Highland Brigade.

'*We're foot-slog-slog-slog-sloggin' over Africa/Foot-slog-slog-slog-sloggin' over Africa/(Boots-boots-boots-boots-movin' up and down again!)/There's no discharge in the war!*' So wrote Rudyard Kipling to describe the long marches made through the heat and the dust as the British Army pursued the elusive Boer commandos. At least the Pipes and Drums provided some relief to the endless trudge. (IWM Q72134)

A far cry from the spick and span troops who had arrived at the Cape short months before: a kilt-apron covers the sporran, a slouch hat gives some protection from sun and rain, the equipment is no longer white and spats have been replaced by rudimentary puttees. But there can be no doubt the Argylls mean business. (IWM Q71940)

The Volunteer (later Territorial) Battalions of the Regiment produced three Volunteer Service Companies, which went out to reinforce the 1st Battalion in 1900, 1901 and 1902. Here the 1st Volunteer Service Company raised in 1900 is drawn up in the snow on the Upper Square, Stirling Castle. The families look on in the background. This was the first occasion but by no means the last that the Regular Battalion called on the Volunteers, and their successors the Territorials, for support.

The 4th Volunteer Battalion (later 7th Argyll & Sutherland Highlanders) detachment for the 2nd Active Service Company of 1901. Each company served for a year although a number of men elected to stay on. The slouch hat has now replaced the helmet, obviously newly issued, as is the tunic which has not been cut away in front. (39)

The Regimental Depot Church Parade outside the King's Chapel, Stirling Castle, in August 1901. Highland regiments have always been noted for the variety in their Orders of Dress but the widespread stations of the regiment have produced a particularly remarkable collection of uniforms on this occasion. Neither slouch hat nor tropical helmet seem entirely appropriate for Stirling's weather.

The 3rd Militia Battalion marching into camp. Both Militia Battalions of the Regiment saw service in South Africa; the 3rd, under command of the Duke of Montrose, from February 1902 onwards. On arrival it was split into detachments with much of its time garrisoning blockhouses, often under heavy sniping in an area which was later revealed to harbour some 1,200 Boers. It embarked for the UK in September of the same year having lost one officer and eight men on operations.

Above: The latter part of the war was spent in corralling the elusive Boer commandos between lines of blockhouses, such as the one seen here, occupied by men of the 3rd Militia Battalion. When enemy fire became too hot, the garrison would retire inside the building and fire from the embrasures.

Left: Local expeditions after game provided some relief to the monotony and a welcome addition to the rations. As so often in war, ninety-five per cent of the time was passed in total boredom with the remaining five per cent too exciting for comfort!

Left: The 4th Militia Battalion arrived in February 1900 and served until July 1901 losing twenty-three men. It spent most of the time on lines of communication but was involved in a number of small actions, particularly involving its Mounted Infantry Troop. Col. Douglas-Dick was awarded the CB, Lt-Col. M.D. Campbell the DSO and Colour Sergeants J. Mackie and J. Mitchell both received the DCM, while eleven members of the Battalion were Mentioned in Despatches.

Below: Men from 'E' Company of the 1st Battalion man a blockhouse in the final stages of the war. By its end, the 91st had lost ninety-three officers and men killed in action and a further fifty-six dead through accident or disease.

On return from South Africa, the Battalion quickly returned to peacetime routine, as did the rest of the Army. We'd had no end of a lesson in South Africa but it did us little good some twelve years later. This group of the officers of the 1st Battalion was taken *c.*1908, Lt-Col. R.L.E. McKerrell in command.

The 1st Battalion provided the Royal Guard at Balmoral for the newly crowned King Edward VII in 1902; they are here seen drawn up on parade in the Barrack Square, Ballater.

Judging the Best Dressed Soldier at the 93rd's Battalion Games at Poona in 1904. The inspecting officer's dog inspects from the rear.

Officers of the 93rd at the Centenary Ball, Calcutta, 1903. It was a fancy of the smarter regiments that the officers on such an occasion should all dress alike in period uniforms. This magnificent turnout is a figment of imagination since the 93rd never dressed in this fashion but the effect is undoubtedly impressive.

A carefully posed photograph of the 2nd Battalion Sergeants' Mess, Poona, 1906. Note the smartly dressed Indian servants and the several-weeks-old newspapers and magazines from home, which are nevertheless being eagerly devoured.

A home from home; these soldiers of the 93rd in India have made a determined effort to improve the austere barrack room with pictures, printed dadoes and a colourful coverlet – all no doubt folded away for room inspection.

The 1st Battalion on the march from Longmoor to Aldershot in June 1904. The Pioneer Section followed by the Pipes and Drums lead the column. The men still wear the slouch hat as issued for the war in South Africa but it is now adorned with a white hackle and the khaki kilt-apron has been discarded.

A family picnic for the Permanent Staff of the 4th Militia Battalion at Irvine in Ayrshire, 1904. Some, it will be noted, have brought their bicycles, still a recent invention and an object of admiration; all are splendidly dressed although keeping the children from getting dirty on such an occasion must have been a constant effort.

L/Cpl Cruikshank on guard; men of the 1st Battalion guard the Main Gate entrance to the Gravesend Barracks *c.*1904. After a hundred years, the recruiting problem is still with us!

The 2nd Battalion Mounted Infantry Section, India, 1906. After the Boer War, each infantry battalion included a mounted section who acted much as the later Recce Platoon. In 1903 the 1st Battalion provided a Mounted Escort to Princess Louise at Longmoor, an unusual and possibly unique task for an Infantry Regiment.

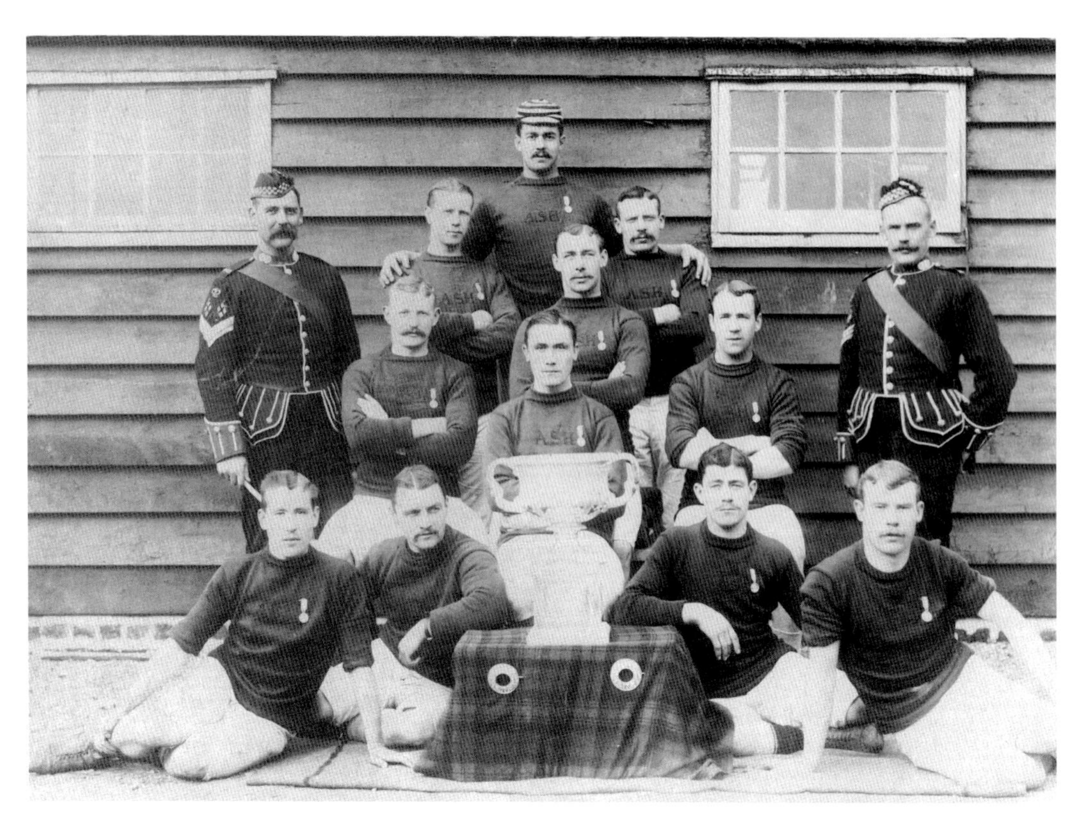

Opposite above: Football has always played an important part in regimental life. The 2nd Battalion won the Army Cup in 1908. The victorious team line up for their photograph with Capt. McCandlish, the officer in charge of the team, seated in the centre with the Captain, L/Cpl J. MacMillan. Their record was played sixteen, won fourteen, drawn two, goals for eighty-seven, against twelve.

Opposite below: Pipe Major Archibald Ferguson of the 93rd conducting a class for pipers of the 27th Punjabis and the Raja of Karpurthala's Imperial Service Infantry. The pipes have always been popular with Indian and Arab armies and continue so today. Both the modern Indian and Pakistan armies have many pipe bands which play a mixture of Scottish and local airs.

Right: The long and short of it; a boy bandsman (4ft 3½ in) and the bass drummer (6ft 1½ in), 1909. Officers of the Regiment took pride in producing suitable animal pelts for the drummers.

Right: Sgt-Maj. Heatley of the 91st and his unique cane. When the 91st were returning from South Africa in 1802, a narwhal attacked the troopship and left its tusk embedded in the ship's timbers. It was made into a cane which was carried through the campaign in the Peninsula and at Waterloo by its owner, Alexander Maclean, and on his death in 1869 it was presented to the regiment. Embellished with a gold band engraved with the 91st's Battle Honours, it was carried for many years by the current Sergeant Major. It is now to be seen in the Regimental Museum in Stirling Castle.

The Opening of Parliament at Valetta, Malta, October 1909. The Guard of Honour, found by the 91st, march off at the conclusion of the ceremony. The Palace Guard, seen at the top right of the photograph, are fallen in, in front of the Governor's Palace.

A Guard of Honour under Capt. D.J. Glasfurd of the 1st Battalion receives Gen. Sir Ian Hamilton, newly appointed Commander-in-Chief, Mediterranean, on his arrival in Malta, October 1910. Sir Ian, a Gordon Highlander, was to command the ill-starred Gallipoli Expedition a few years later, in which the 5th Battalion was to take part.

A 93rd musical line-up. Left to right: Pipe Major J. Lawrie, Bandmaster F.J. Ricketts, Band Sergeant T. Marriott, Drum Major R.P. MacTavish. Bandmaster Ricketts, who wrote under the name of Kenneth Alford, was a noted composer of marches, among the best known being 'The Thin Red Line' and 'Colonel Bogey'. He ended his career as Lt-Col., Director of Music, Royal Marines. Drummie McTavish was a famous regimental figure and a renowned athlete. Originally enlisted in the 91st in 1908, he served 1914–18 as Drum Major of the Tyneside Scottish before returning to the Argylls, in which his father, uncle and two brothers also served, in 1919. Having played for Newcastle United, he was in the Army football teams of 1920, 1922 and 1923. He died in 1984 at the age of ninety. Pipe Major Lawrie was a noted piper; he won the Gold Medal at the Northern Meeting, Inverness, in 1913. This Gold Medal, awarded by The Highland Society of London, along with that at the Argyllshire Gathering in Oban, holds Olympic status in the world of piping. It had previously been won in 1910 by Pipe Major Willie Lawrie of the 8th Battalion and was won subsequently in 1919 by Pipe Major Willie Gray of the Glasgow Police, formerly of the regiment, by the then Cpl Andrew Pitkeathly in 1949 and by Pipe Major Ronnie MacCallum of the 8th Battalion in 1951.

A Regimental Dinner, 1912, for veterans of Balaklava and the Crimea. Bandmaster Ricketts is in the foreground.

The 5th (Renfrewshire) Battalion, in company with a large number of other TA Battalions, was presented with new colours by King Edward VII in the grounds of Windsor Castle in 1912. The Ensigns are Lt Donald Main (left), whose family has given several generations of service to the regiment, and Lt Reid Kerr (right).

The old and bold; Argyll & Sutherland Highlander In-Pensioners of The Royal Hospital Chelsea, 1912.

The other end of the age spectrum. Children of the Regiment at Queen Victoria School, Dunblane. Queen Victoria School was established in 1908 as a memorial to the Queen. Located in Dunblane, Perthshire, it was to cater for the children of Scottish servicemen. Originally for boys only, it now includes girls as well.

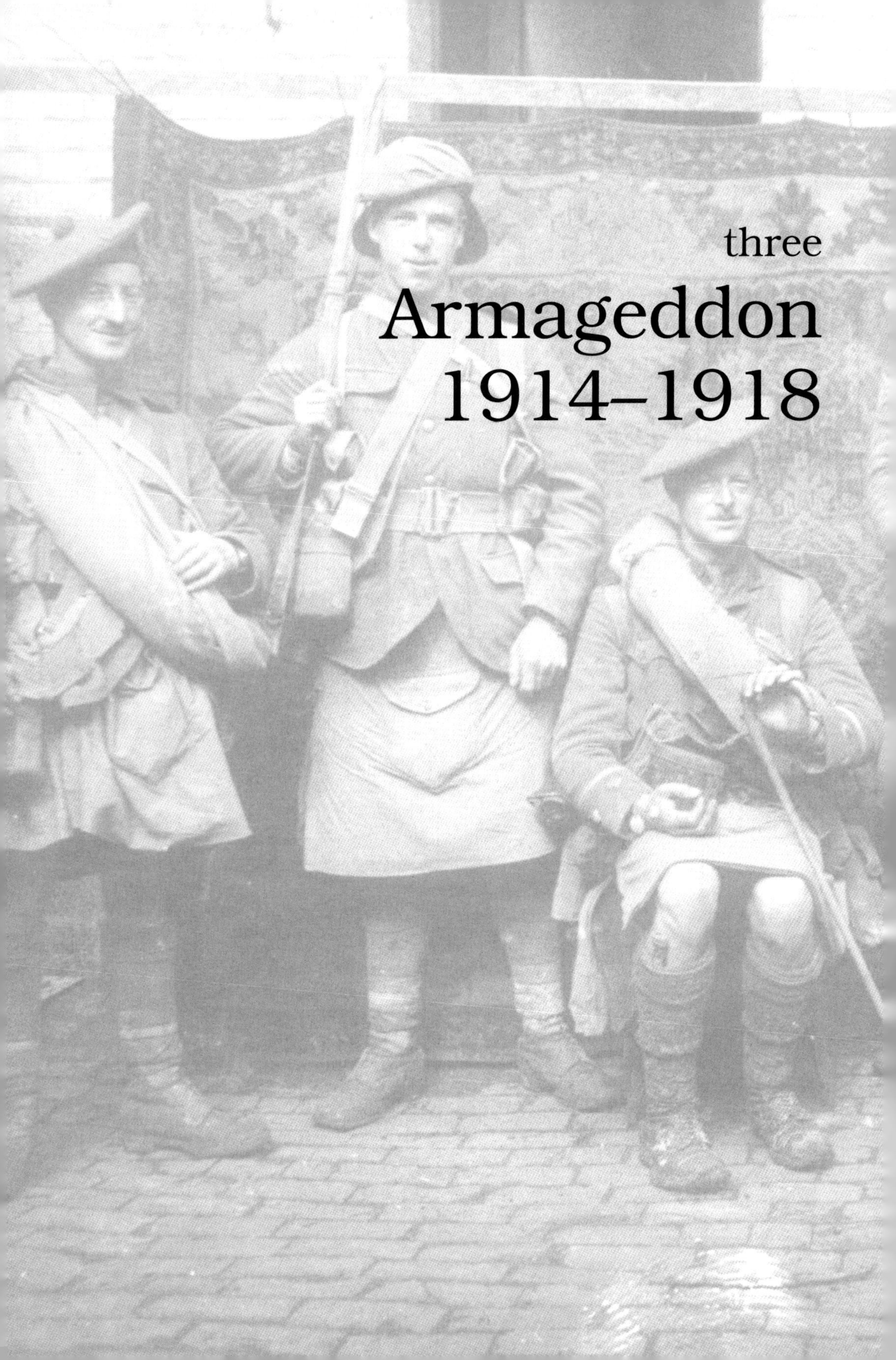

three

Armageddon 1914–1918

The First World War of 1914–18 was to be a conflict the like of which the world had never seen before. By its end, the regiment had embodied 27 battalions which served in Egypt, Palestine, Macedonia, Gallipoli, Italy and, above all, in France and Flanders. Here, Piper Murray of the 6th Renfrewshire TA Battalion plays to let the enemy know who they are up against.

A Group of officers of the 8th (Argyllshire) Battalion TF on mobilisation at annual camp, August 1914. On the extreme left is Lt James Taylor from Southend, Argyll, who had served with the 1st Battalion in South Africa as a Colour Sergeant and whose son Hamish was to command the same Battalion with distinction in the Second World War. Next to him is the Quartermaster, then Lt (later Maj.) Andrew Lockie, while the figure in the feather bonnet is Capt. J.A.L. Campbell of Jura, 'Jura Jock', the regular Adjutant.

In more warlike attire, Niall, 10th Duke of Argyll, poses with the officers of the 8th Battalion, Dunoon, 1914. In command is Campbell of Kilberry, a noted piping enthusiast, who had as his Pipe Major the famous Willie Lawrie from Ballachulish, a great character and composer. Among the latter's remarks which deserve preservation is his disgusted comment about life in the trenches: 'This iss no' the life for a Pipe Major at all; stuck like a bluidy rat in a drainpipe!'

A Battalion of the Regiment marches towards the trenches. Pipers lead the men, followed by the CO with his Bugler. A picture like this has special poignancy in view of the fact that the same battalion leaving the trenches will be many fewer in number.

A confident-looking group in the trenches; note the equipment hanging ready to hand and the shelf containing rudimentary hand-grenades just below the parapet. Life in the open was surprisingly healthy if not exactly comfortable and once they had got themselves organised, the Jocks survived it remarkably well. Shelling, gas and enemy snipers were another matter.

Above: Probably the most extreme of all the horrors produced by the First World War was gas. At first there was no protection and troops depended on motorcyclist's goggles and a pad soaked in their own urine until proper gas masks could be developed.

Right: Another new weapon was the aeroplane; a Sergeant of the 93rd with a Vickers Medium Machine Gun mounted to counter this new menace.

Sanitation in the trenches was a constant problem: there were few chances for washing; well-fed rats swarmed everywhere and there were lice and other vermin to contend with. Here a Jock prepares to spray the trenches with disinfectant. It is a remarkable fact, however, that life in the trenches was, physically, apart from the attentions of the enemy, a remarkably healthy one.

The ever popular char and wad: Jocks brew up in the trenches. Note the cap comforters worn as an alternative to the glengarry at this stage of the war, when the steel helmet had yet to make an appearance.

Right: A remarkable trio of Argyll subalterns; Lt W.D. Bissett, centre, and Lt J. Buchan, right, were both to win the Victoria Cross, Bissett with the 6th Battalion and Buchan with the 7th.

Below: A cheerful group from the 8th Battalion. The khaki TOS was another new feature of the war, a special early version worn by the 8th was known after its inventor, Col. Campbell of Inverneill, as the 'Inverneill Bonnet'. This was reversible and could be either blue or khaki.

Left: The bucket with holes punched in its sides to make a brazier provides the only form of central heating for this dugout carved out of the side of the trench to give some rudimentary shelter from the worst of the elements.

Below: The historic meeting of the 91st and 93rd at Armentières in June 1915. Seated in the centre, Lt-Col. Gore (91st) (TOS) and Lt-Col. Kirk (91st) (Glengarry). Several of the junior officers survived the war and went on to command Battalions of the Regiment – among them Capt. Hay Young, extreme left, back row, who commanded the 93rd on the Frontier in 1937 and his successor, Lt Greenfield, sitting front row, second from right. Famous member of an extended regimental family is Capt. Harry Clark, standing in the second row, second from right with, on his right, 2nd-Lt 'Copper' Buchanan, taken prisoner in France in 1940 as CO of the 7th Battalion, whose three sons also served in the Argylls.

Pipers of the 5th Battalion at revolver target practice, Gaza, 1917. Note the size of the TOS, a far cry from the shrunken and shapeless versions resembling a cowpat seen all too often today!

A bathing parade for the 1st Battalion at Stavros – a welcome cooling off.

Men of the 1st Battalion at bayonet training, 1917. Instructors insisted that the thrust was accompanied by a bloodcurdling yell.

A jovial group of the 93rd on the Western Front. The sheepskin fleeces were introduced during the first winter of the war in order to help the troops survive winter living in the trenches. Unfortunately, although warm, they served as an ideal breeding ground for lice and had to be discarded.

Men of the 1st Battalion guard a party of Bulgar prisoners, taken on the Struma. The Battalion, which had previously served on the Western Front, moved to Macedonia in December 1915 to face the Bulgars, allies of the Turks, and remained fighting on that front until the Armistice. Their losses were not inconsiderable but the most dangerous enemy was malaria.

The war over, the 1st Battalion found itself in the Turkish capital, Constantinople, where it was tasked with finding the guard for GHQ and the Commander-in-Chief. Here, the Transport Section is seen lined up with its mule-drawn limbers.

four

The uneasy pause 1918–1939

Above: As peacetime routine was resumed, the 91st was posted to India. The Prince of Wales inspects a Guard from the 1st Battalion in Poona, 19 November 1921, commanded by Capt. C.B. Robertson, father of Col. Ian Robertson LVO, who also served with distinction in the regiment. The Prince's combination of Tropical and Home Service uniform earned him a rocket from his father.

Left: In 1924 the 91st moved to Egypt. Here a sentry of the 1st Battalion stands guard over the barracks in Cairo. Later that year trouble broke out in the Sudan, where Egyptian troops had become mutinous, and the Battalion was called out on active service once more in order to restore the situation.

Right: An attempt to enforce the disarming of two Egyptian battalions led to a vicious action in which one officer and five other ranks were killed and seven wounded. The Acting CO, Maj. J.R. Couper, was awarded the DSO and Privates G. MacLeod (left) and J. Wright (right) received Military Medals. Not shown here is Capt. T. Kerr who was awarded a bar to his Military Cross.

Below: On 28 April, 1926 in Cairo, new colours were presented to the 1st Battalion by Lord Lloyd, the British High Commissioner. Here, the Escort to the Colours under command of Maj. G.F. Connal-Rowan troop the colours in front of the Battalion. The Ensigns were Lieutenants C. Hetherwick MC and R.G. Hyde. This was the first occasion since the end of the war that the 91st had paraded in white spats.

The old and new colours of the 91st at the Citadel, Cairo, April 1926. The CO in the picture was Lt-Col. G.W. Muir whose son, Maj. Kenny Muir, was to win a posthumous Victoria Cross with the 1st Battalion in Korea.

The Battalion transport drawn up on the Barrack Square, Cairo, 1927. It is hard to realise now the impact of mechanisation nor how relatively recently it took place, overturning, as it did, the practice of centuries.

The Argylls march past the Commander-in-Chief. The date and location of this picture are unknown but it is so atmospheric as to merit inclusion. The orderly with the Union Flag denotes the status of the inspection officer. It is either early morning or late evening, as shown by the long shadows, but although the worst of the heat is avoided, the dust is rising as the long lines swing past. The date must be early 1920s as the Battalion is still in boots and puttees.

A business like guard for HM the King, found by the 2nd Battalion, Aldershot, 1923. Note that the 93rd were wearing a white hackle in the TOS at this time.

A very smart Guard of Honour with the Pipes and Drums and Military Band of the 93rd drawn up to greet Princess Louise on her arrival at Parkhurst, 1926.

HRH Princess Louise, Duchess of Argyll, presents colours to the 2nd Battalion, Isle of Wight, 1926.

Parkhurst, 1926. HRH Princess Louise inspects the parade accompanied by the CO, Lt-Col. James DSO. In front, the Orderly Officer in full dress is Capt. G.H.A. MacMillan MC, later to become Gen. Sir Gordon MacMillan of MacMillan and Knap, Chief of the Clan MacMillan and Colonel of the Regiment.

Her Royal Highness with the Warrant Officers and Sergeants; on her right, the famous RSM 'Boss' McKay MC; on her left, Bandmaster Ricketts. On the RSM's right is the CO, Lt-Col. C.P. James DSO, and on his right, RQMS Duncan MC MM. Maj.-Gen. Sir A. Wilson, Colonel of the Regiment and father and grandfather of distinguished Argyll officers, is on the Bandmaster's left.

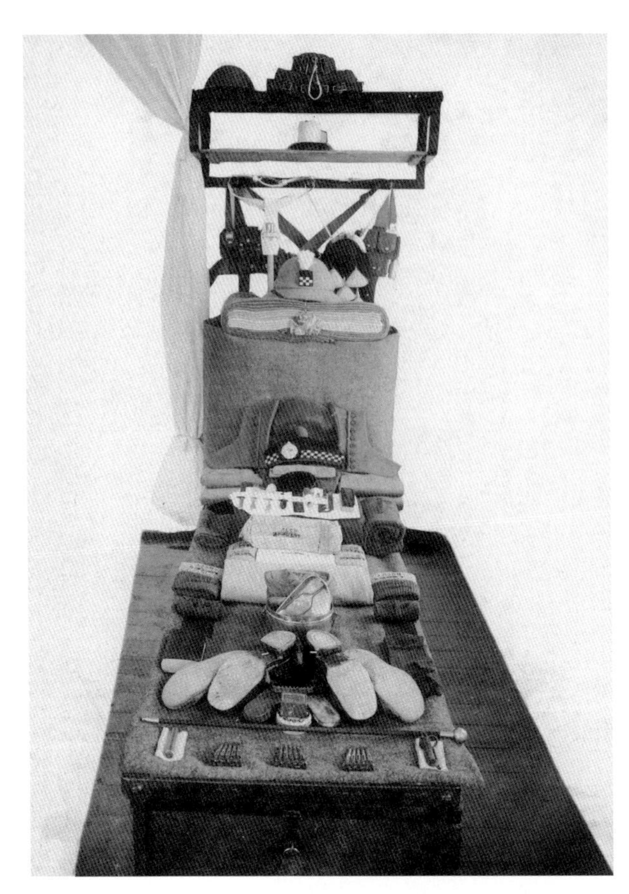

Left: A familiar sight? Kit layout for inspection, 2nd Battalion, 1926. It all looks much the same as ever but note the solar topee with white hackle and the swagger cane for walking out.

Below: Princess Louise with the Officers of the 93rd, 1926. Flanked as before by Lt-Col. James and Gen. Wilson, other notables include second left, front row, the General's son Maj. R.G. Wilson DSO, and in the back row in full dress Capt. G.H.A. MacMillan MC, with Capt. Ian Stewart OBE MC on his immediate right and second right Capt. H.A. Campbell, grandfather of today's Regimental Secretary.

Right: A sentry on the main gate, Tientsin, 1929. The sub-zero temperatures required special clothing; note the heavy overcoat with fur collar, the fur hat with regimental collar badge in front, the gloves and special boots.

Below: A section of the 93rd, in shirtsleeve Battle Order, patrol the streets of Shanghai to protect the Japanese Quarter in 1932. If winters were cold, the summers went to the opposite extreme.

Dead cool! L/Cpl W. Jordan all set to walk out in his civilian suit, a privilege granted to those of good character.

Equally, unlike the present, many preferred to walk out in their best uniform. It is sad that today the Services are virtually unseen on the streets; uniform was a source of pride to the wearer, an attraction to the opposite sex and a potent recruiter.

A Group of off-duty Jocks outside the Camp Cinema, Shanghai, *c.*1933. The fur hats were obviously popular.

Drum Major John Seton DCM, a former Regular Argyll, was Drum Major of the 8th (Argyllshire) Battalion from 1935–37. A Govan policeman who lost two fingers in a bomb explosion, he was the world authority on Pipe Band drumming. His name will always be remembered as a co-author, with Pipe Major William Gray, also late of the 93rd, of the *Bagpipe and Drum Tutor*, the first occasion on which instruction on combined piping and drumming had ever been set down in print. Previously Pipe Major of the City of Glasgow Police, Gray had been Pipe Major of the 2nd Battalion throughout the First World War, a unique appointment for a non-regular soldier.

Military tattoos were very much a part of peacetime soldiering. The last occasion that a whole Battalion of the Regiment paraded in the old, scarlet full-dress was here at the Tidworth Tattoo of 1935. It is indeed sad that such a magnificent sight was never to be seen again.

Maj. Ian Stewart of Achnacone OBE MC with senior NCOs of the Depot, Stirling Castle. Achnacone was later to command the 2nd Battalion during the campaign against the Japanese in Malaya and Singapore. On his right is RSM J. Kenny and on his left ORQMS J. Carmichael. Note the pattern of blue patrol with open collar, shirt and tie.

In 1937 the 93rd were engaged in an expedition to subdue the rebellious Faqir of Ipi and his supporters in the precipitous mountains of Waziristan on the North-West Frontier. Air support was important and here an RAF aircraft drops supplies to the Battalion.

A patrol sets out; the officer is Lt – later Brigadier – Ted Snowball OBE, whose son, Andrew, was to serve with the regiment in Northern Ireland. Shortly after this photo was taken, Lt Snowball was shot through the shoulder. He went on to command the 6th Seaforth in North-West Europe and was CO of the 8th Battalion after the war. He retired in 1968 as a Brigadier and died in 1987.

Prisoners under guard, Arsal Kot, Waziristan Operations, 1937. The 2nd Battalion sustained several casualties against an enemy who knew every inch of the ground and for whom warfare was an essential part of life.

Machine Gun Post guarding Bahadur Camp. These camps were tactical since the enemy sniped constantly at night and were capable of mounting an attack if security was lax.

Although apparently strong enough, the small garrison of such a permanent picquet as this could never relax. Hidden eyes watched their every move and a bullet or a swift stabbing rush would follow any failure to maintain maximum alert.

Behind the scanty protection of its sangar – piled up boulders, since digging in was impossible in such terrain – a .303 Vickers Machine Gun guards a hilltop picquet, the crew on the alert.

The 2nd Battalion practise with their new Carden Lloyd Carriers – forerunners of the later Bren Gun Carrier.

In the Coronation Year of 1937, the 8th Battalion became the first Territorials to find the Royal Guard for Holyrood Palace; the Guard Commander was Capt. Lorne Campbell (later Brigadier VC DSO OBE TD) with Lt Paul Tress as 2 i/c. At the right-hand end of the rear rank is Pte Jimmy Masterton of Dunoon, later well known as 'The Brush' and RSM of the 1st Battalion in the mid-1950s.

five

All to do again 1939–1945

Cheerful Jocks of the 7th Battalion in France in 1940, as part of the 51st Highland Division. In June that year they received the full thrust of the German *Blitzkrieg* and, after a gallant defence against overwhelming odds at Franleu, most of the Battalion's survivors were taken prisoner. (IWM F4732)

Sgt (later Maj.) 'Sandy Blood' MacDonald and L/Cpl Willy Kemp of the 8th Battalion examine their Military Medals, awarded for their escape along with Pte 'Ginger' Wilson in 1940. All three came from North Argyll and their conversation in Gaelic bemused the Germans they met into believing they must be Russian, permitting their successful escape into Vichy France and thence to Spain. MacDonald was a son of 'The Blood' – the renowned CSM John MacDonald MC DCM of Ballachulish.

L/Cpl Inch (left) and Sgt Brown (right) lead a long column of Italian prisoners taken by the 1st Battalion at Sidi Barrani in December 1940. Cpl Inch was killed in action in September 1940 but Sgt Brown, who had joined the regiment as a bandboy, is now Lt-Col. Andrew Brown MBE. (IWM A-4-9 33/91)

Gunflashes light up the horizon on 23 October 1942, as the Battle of El Alamein opens. The new 51st Highland Division was in the forefront of the attack, reconstituted after St Valéry from the second-line 9th Scottish Division, which had been formed from duplicate battalions of those in the old 51st. Led by their pipers, the 7th/10th Battalion of the Argylls were to extract a notable revenge, fighting across the desert, Sicily and North-West Europe until the German surrender in 1945. (IWM E18465)

Longstop Hill barred the 1st Army's path to Tunis; strongly held, it dominated the open plain beneath. The task of its capture was given to the 8th (Argyllshire) Battalion. Shortly after this picture of the advancing Battalion HQ was taken, it and the CO were wiped out by German shell and mortar fire. But the 8th pressed on and in an epic action in which Maj. Jack Anderson won the Victoria Cross, took the hill against all odds and held it. (IWM NA2235)

After their period on the north-west Frontier, the 93rd moved to Singapore. The early years of the war left the garrison alone, inducing, perhaps, a false sense of security. But their CO, Lt-Col. Ian Stewart of Achnacone, was under no false illusions. While other battalions kept to their peacetime routine, he drove his battalion hard. (IWM K594)

They trained in the jungle and muddy mangrove swamps until they were totally familiar with the difficult terrain. When, in 1942, the Japanese attacked, the 93rd was one of the few units that was able to meet them on equal terms. (IWM K582)

The Battalion had managed to acquire a troop of armoured cars which played a vital role in defending the few roads through the jungle that formed the key to the defence. Fighting hard, the Argylls were forced back from the mainland; they covered the final withdrawal of the Allied troops across the causeway into Singapore Island where, along with the rest of the defenders, they were forced to surrender. Long years of captivity followed as slave labourers to the Japanese, but the name of the 93rd and their epic fight was to endure. (IWM FE352)

On his motorcycle, in charge of the armoured cars on a training exercise, is the MTO, Capt. Tam Slessor. Promoted from the ranks, he survived the years of captivity to become successively 2 i/c of the 1st Battalion before becoming Commandant of the School of Army Physical Training with the rank of Lieutenant Colonel. On retirement he became Regimental Secretary. (IWM FE349)

Following the capture of the 93rd in Singapore in 1942, the 11th Battalion, originally the duplicate battalion of the 8th, took on the identity of the former 2nd Battalion and, as such, formed part of the 15th Scottish Division which landed in Normandy shortly after D-Day and fought its way into Germany. Here, men of 'C' Company, led by Maj. Graham Graham of Redknock, follow their piper out of the line. (IWM B5988)

2nd Argylls move up to the attack carried on Churchill tanks of the Guards Armoured Division. From its landing in France until he was wounded in early August, the 15th Scottish Division was commanded by Gen. Gordon MacMillan of the Regiment. (IWM B12026)

The 2nd Battalion were in the forefront of the 15th Division's attack across the Rhine against stiff opposition, which they successfully overcame before pressing on. Here, men of the Argylls move up through Celle with only another 20 miles to go to the Elbe. The end is in sight.

At the close of hostilities, the 8th Battalion occupied Austria with the 78th Division. It was a happy change, marred only by the unpleasant task of handing over a surrendered Cossack SS Division to the Russians. Drill and ceremonial featured once again and the 8th were soon properly turned out as Highlanders should be, in the kilts which had been subscribed for them by the people of Argyll when the Government withdrew the official issue at the beginning of the war. The colours were sent for and here the Colour Party is formed up outside the Battalion's barracks in Linz.

As ever with the 8th, the Pipes and Drums were of a high standard and played a major part in the life of the Battalion. Here they play in the town, which shows signs of war, with the snow-clad mountains behind. The Pipe President was Capt. James Campbell of the Kilberry family, well known as piping authorities, and the Pipe Major was Pipe Major Lawrence Georgeson.

Longstop Day, 23 April 1946; the 8th Battalion celebrate the third anniversary of their great Tunisian battle. The CO, Lt-Col. George Malcolm of Poltalloch who, before the war, had served as regular Adjutant of the Battalion is mounted at the head of the parade.

In 1947 the regiment was one of the very first to be honoured by HRH Princess Elizabeth becoming Colonel-in-Chief; Her Majesty has now served in that capacity for over half a century. She visited the 1st Battalion in June 1949 in Colchester and is here seen with the officers. On her right is Lt-Col. Cluny Macpherson, commanding; on her left, Lt-Gen. Sir Gordon MacMillan of MacMillan KCB CBE DSO MC, Colonel of the Regiment. The two officers in Service Dress flanking each end of the second row are, on the left, Lt John Slim, son of the Field Marshal, who was later to command the 22nd SAS, and on the right, 2nd-Lt A.C.S. Boswell later Lt-Gen. Sir Alexander Boswell KCB CBE, Colonel of the Regiment.

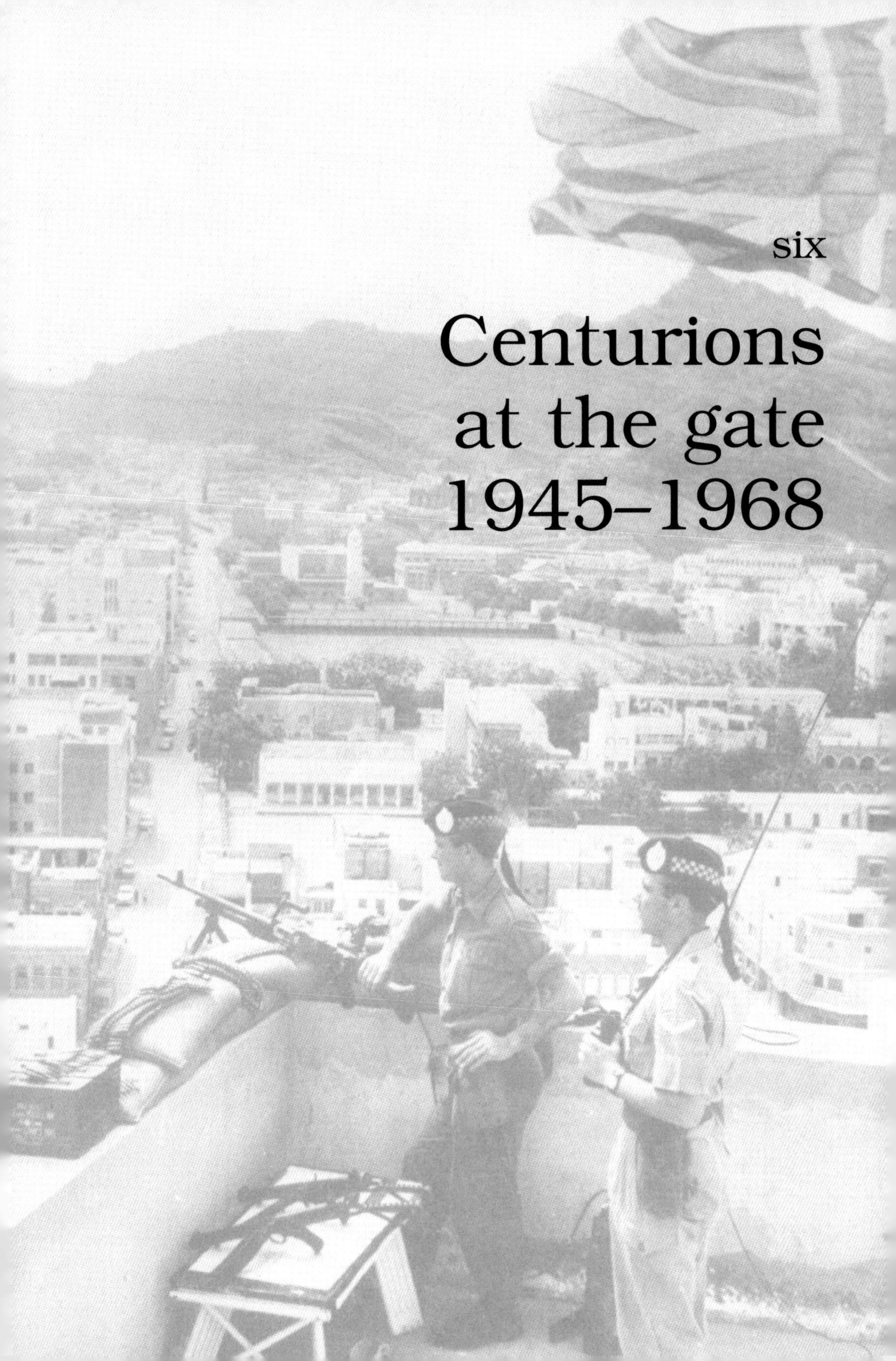

six

Centurions at the gate 1945–1968

Following the end of the war, the 1st Battalion found itself in Palestine with a very unpleasant job of attempting to counter Jewish terrorist gangs and then to keep the peace between Jew and Arab. For the latter part of their tour, the GOC was Gen. MacMillan for whom the 1st Battalion found an escort for his personal protection.

The RSO Capt. Nigel Crowe leads a convoy down the road, ready for ambush, mine or grenade. Nigel Crowe was later 2 i/c of the Battalion under Lt-Col. Mitchell in Aden; an Arabic speaker, after retirement from the British Army he served in the post-Independence Rhodesian Forces.

CSM Brown and his carrier patrol of 'C' Company ready to move off; a curfew was being applied after the notorious blowing-up of the King David Hotel which housed GHQ in Jerusalem; men of the 1st Battalion had been early on the scene to render what aid they could to the trapped and injured.

The curfew is in force as Argylls patrol the empty streets; the regiment was to carry out similar tasks on many occasions during the years to come in Egypt, Cyprus, Aden, Northern Ireland and Iraq.

Returning fire; an escort comes under fire from an Arab ambush on the Jaffa-Tel Aviv border. One man, Pte Kane, was killed and another, Pte Shaw, wounded; in the engagement four Arabs were killed and a dozen wounded.

'A' company mounted up and ready to go, Lydda, 1948. By now there was a war raging between Jew and Arab with the British in the middle. Opposing gangs were now some 500 strong and the Argylls were frequently under heavy fire.

In 1947 with the abolition of 2nd Battalion, the 93rd was officially amalgamated with the 91st, which now incorporated both its founding regiments. The last colours of the 93rd were laid up in Stirling Castle with due ceremony. Here, they are marched up under an escort with fixed bayonets from the Castle Esplanade.

In 1950 the 1st Battalion was sent, as part of the Commonwealth Brigade, to fight the Communists alongside the Americans in Korea as part of a United Nations force. Here, on 25 August 1950, men of the Argylls march along the Hong Kong quayside to embark on the cruiser HMS *Ceylon* which was to take them to war yet again.

Above: Their most famous action was that of Hill 282, less than a month after their arrival, when, although forced off the hill by misdirected American bombing, they reoccupied the position and fought off furious enemy onslaughts. The counter-attack was led by the Battalion 2 i/c, Maj. Kenny Muir, who died at the head of his men, winning the regiment's last VC. Peter Archer's painting was done with the help of several actual participants in the battle.

Left: The strain of battle shows as his men carry the wounded Lt Jock Edington off Hill 282. Although now largely forgotten, the Korean War was a fierce and nasty war fought largely by reservists and National Servicemen; they did not let the regiment down.

Right: The extra firepower of machine guns played a vital role in fending off the massed suicide attacks by the Chinese and North Koreans. An MMG detachment of the 1st Battalion waits, ready for anything.

Below: The scene as Argyll wounded support each other off Hill 282. The Battalion sustained 6 officers and 29 other ranks killed and 10 officers and 126 other ranks wounded during the Korean War in which a further 9 other ranks were killed and 45 wounded while serving with The King's Own Scottish Borderers who had followed the Argylls to Korea. For its services, the regiment was awarded the Battle Honours 'Pakchon' and 'Korea 1950–51'.

Left: On their return to the UK in September 1952 the Battalion, now under the command of Lt-Col. Jim Church MC, received a heroes' welcome. It marched down Edinburgh's Princes Street, the salute being taken by the Lord Provost and the GOC Scotland. Leading the column was their newly-presented Shetland Pony mascot, the famous 'Cruachan II'.

Below: In 1953 the 1st Battalion provided extras for Walt Disney's film *Rob Roy, The Highland Rogue* starring Richard Todd. According to accounts, all concerned thoroughly enjoyed the experience although over-enthusiasm led to some of the battles on screen becoming distressingly realistic.

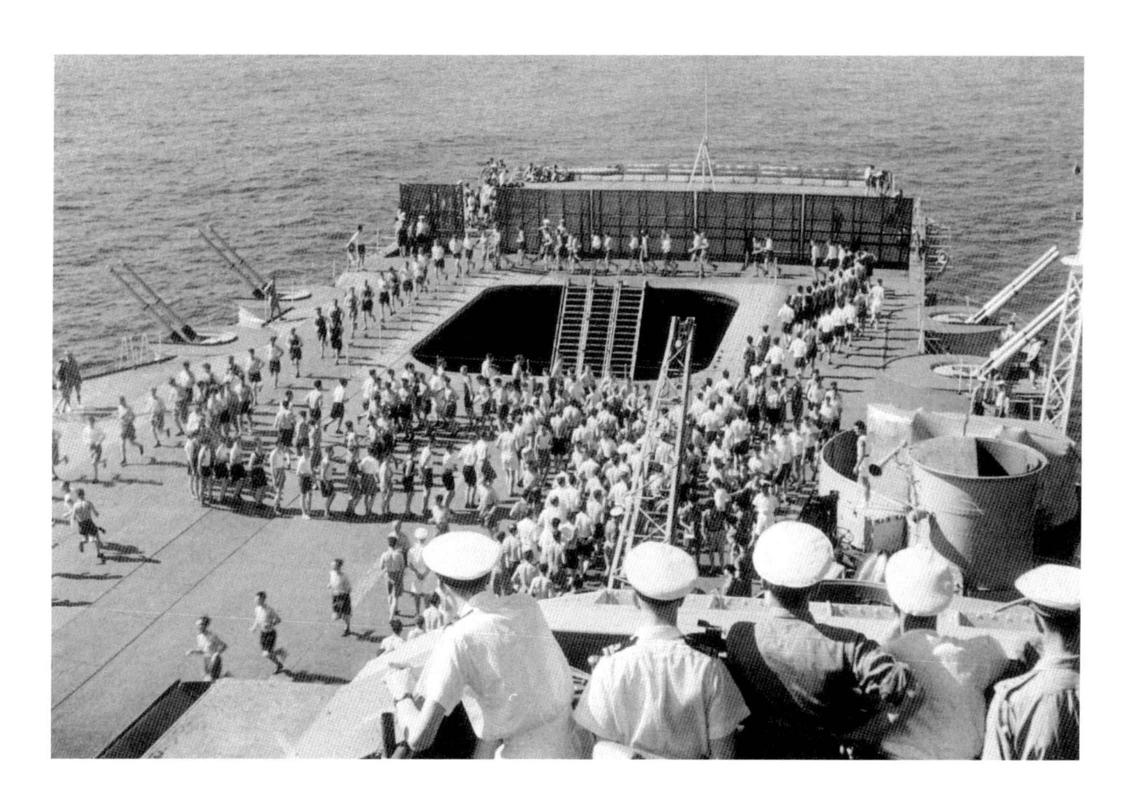

Above: In October 1953 the 1st Battalion was off again – this time to British Guiana, transported by HMS *Implacable* whose Captain, Capt. Alan Campbell OBE RN, was the son of a previous CO of the 8th Battalion and a brother of Brigadier Lorne Campbell VC. In 1940, as Naval Liaison Officer, he had been responsible for the Navy's rescue of the remnants of the 8th from the port of Le Havre.

Right: The Battalion was required to keep an unsettled political situation in check. In the event there was little serious violence, thanks no doubt at least in part to the Argylls' presence. Here shown is a carrier patrol moving through a village. With few exceptions, the population was extremely friendly.

Lt-Col. Barclay Pearson DSO, leads the Battalion on a flag march through the capital of British Guiana, Georgetown, following the Queen's Birthday Parade in front of the Governor, April 1954. Immediately behind him is the legendary RSM Paddy Boyde MBE DCM.

In 1956 the 1st Battalion took part in the abortive Suez operation. Here, carriers of the Anti-Tank Platoon line up outside a block of flats on Port Said's waterfront.

Above and below: The Battle Honour 'Balaklava' has always been a particular source of pride to the regiment as the only infantry regiment to be so honoured. It commemorates the incident in the Crimean War when the 93rd remained in line to repel the charge of the Russian Cavalry without deigning to form square. A famous picture was painted by Robert Gibb, a schoolmaster in Dunoon, depicting the scene. As part of the centenary celebrations in Stirling it was repeated among other *tableaux vivants* on the stage of the local theatre. Lt Kenneth Maclean takes the part of the officer while Col.-Sgt A. Biggarstaff occupies the same position as his forebear Col.-Sgt Bickerstaff in the actual battle.

In 1959 the 1st Battalion were once more bound for active service, this time in Cyprus where Greek Nationalist terrorists had mounted a campaign in the name of *Enosis* – Independence. Cruachan II came too. He is here seen being embarked on the troopship HMT *Devonshire* which took the Battalion out. From left to right: RSM Jimmy 'The Brush' Masterton; L/Cpl Alex Morrison from Islay, the Pony Major; Piper Harry Oakley and Drum Major Davey Legg whose service had commenced on the North-West Frontier and who became an In-Pensioner of the Royal Hospital, Chelsea.

The Battalion kept up a ceaseless programme of patrols and observation in the mountains with only brief contacts with EOKA who preferred the shot from an ambush or a bomb thrown over a wall. The Machine Gun Platoon enjoy a brief respite with melons!

The Duke of Argyll, whose ancestor had ordered the raising of the Argyllshire Highlanders in 1794 and who himself was a former officer of the 8th Battalion, came to visit the Battalion at Limni Camp while he and the Duchess were enjoying a Mediterranean holiday. He is inspecting the Quarter Guard under command of Sgt 'Big Andra' Gilmour with the CO, Lt-Col. 'Chippy' Anderson.

The biggest operation in which the Battalion took part in Cyprus was 'Operation Kingfisher' in which an equivalent Brigade cordoned and searched a remote mountain valley for several weeks. There were several contacts but no capture of the terrorist leader Gen. Grivas who was the target. Resupply was a problem in the hot and arid hills and once again the troops had recourse to four-legged assistance.

The Governor, Sir Hugh Foot, inspects 'Cruachan II' in his smart regimental saddle-cloth and hot weather haircut. With him, the Pony Major, Lt-Col. Anderson and the 2 i/c, Maj. Tam Slessor. Watching in the background is Mr Rauf, the Pakistani Regimental Contractor whose family had for generations served the regiment in its foreign stations.

The Colonel-in-Chief inspects the Royal Guard at Balmoral in 1964; with Her Majesty is the Guard Commander, Maj. Rio Ritchie MBE MC. Following behind with the Duke of Edinburgh is the Guard 2 i/c, Capt. (later Lt-Col.) Alastair Scott-Elliot.

Above: 1965 found the 1st Battalion in Borneo engaged in the cross-border confrontation with hostile Indonesia. Most of the country was mountainous and covered in thick jungle. Helicopters were extensively used for resupply and for moving troops. A patrol disembarks in an open field with the tall jungle behind.

Right: Tracking enemy infiltrators was a key task, carried out with the help of tracker dogs and native Ibans. Sgt Brian Baty, shown in this photograph, was awarded the Military Medal for his bravery in Borneo; he continued his career in the SAS and retired as a Lieutenant Colonel.

Less of a picnic than might appear; the Pipes and Drums mount a waterborne patrol – a swifter means of progress than cutting a path through the jungle. In the bows, Drum Major Malloch; behind him Cpl McQuaid, the bass-drummer and behind him again, Piper Harry Oakley.

A patrol returns to the company base after several days in the 'ulu', lying up by night and moving by day. The country was thick and precipitous and map-reading as much an art as a science in featureless jungle.

Above: Base was hardly a rest camp; sited on a hilltop with cleared fields of fire and protected by wire against enemy attack, constant watchfulness was called for and there was only limited scope to relax in cramped surroundings.

Right: The Regimental Band in kilt and white spats gives a recital while appreciative villagers look on. The band always played a great part in helping the morale of the troops and fomenting goodwill among the locals and it is indeed sad that it is no more.

Above: Peter Archer's dramatic painting of the scene when the Argylls retook Crater. Here, Col. Mitchell stands by his command vehicle, waiting for reports from the companies, accompanied by his Adjutant, Capt. David Thomson. As 'B' Company move into the attack, checked by their commander, Maj. Paddy Palmer, Pipe Major Ken Robson plays 'Moneymusk,' the Regimental Charge. In spite of dire predictions of high casualties, the operation was a bloodless success, apart from one armed Arab.

Left: With his escort on the lookout, Col. Mitchell drives through the area where the mutinous Arab police had gunned down British soldiers; the reluctant figure besides Col. Colin, with only his shoulder visible, is Superintendent Ibrahim, CO of the mutineers.

Above: Hard and dangerous foot-slogging eventually reasserts British control; tails are well up, however, helped by the resumption, on Col. Mitchell's orders, of the familiar Argyll cap-badge in place of the official and little-liked 'crucified moose' of the Highland Brigade. L/Cpl Edwards from Benbecula leads a 'B' Company patrol through the festering back streets.

Right: The Argylls have laid a firm hand on Crater and, for the moment at least, the Union Flag flies over the town once more.

Continual stopping and searching of passers-by removed the initiative from the terrorists and cut down the movement of illicit grenades and other weapons, although it could not completely remove the constant threat of attack. Dogged perseverance and constant vigilance for long hours was required.

So, too, searching for weapons produced results; here, Maj. Ian Mackay, later awarded the Military Cross for his gallantry in Aden, displays a collection of weapons uncovered by his men.

Crater is surrounded by razor-backed moon-like mountains on which the Argylls, along with the SAS, established Observation Posts from which a constant watch could be kept on the teeming streets and alleyways of the town beneath.

A helicopter brings in much-needed resupply to such a post: radio batteries, food and – above all, in the searing heat – water.

A sentry with a GPMG keeps observation. The heat, the glare, the smell and the long, monotonous hours during which nothing happens do not allow a moment's relaxation.

A patrol covers a street; at any moment a shot can ring out or a grenade come flying through the air; any dropping of a constant guard invites trouble.

Col. Colin Mitchell and his escort outside Battalion HQ, about to set out once more to tour the area. If the Argylls dominated Crater, there was little doubt who dominated the Argylls! Col. Mitchell's award of a mere Mention in Despatches was a petty act of spite both to him and his men.

Salute to the fallen; Capt. Ian Mackay (later Brigadier Ian Mackay CBE MC) salutes the grave of Maj. Bryan Malcolm who, with Privates 'Pocus' Hunter and Johnny Moores, lost his life in the ambush by police mutineers.

Pipe Major Kenneth Robson plays a Salute as RSM McKerron lowers the Argylls' regimental flag for the last time from its position above Battalion HQ. If, in obedience to orders, the Battalion had to withdraw, at least it could do so with fitting defiance. Its action in Crater had restored a fragment of much-needed dignity to the badly battered British Lion.

Pipe Major (later Capt.) Andrew Pitkeathly carrying Her Majesty's pipe banner. He later became the Queen's Personal Piper and was then commissioned as Director of Army Bagpiping. He was a distinguished performer who had the Gold Medal at the Northern Meeting among his many trophies and was a leading judge at senior piping competitions.

A drop in temperature! Black Watch and Argyll recruits at the joint Depot at Stirling Castle manage an immaculate appearance in spite of the wintry weather and the treacherous surface underfoot at their 1960s Passing-Out Parade.

A 1960s photograph of the regiment's Pipe Majors. From left to right: Pipe Major A. Pitkeathly, HM the Queen's Piper; Pipe Major J. Smith, MM; Pipe Major R. MacCallum MBE; Pipe Major K. Robson; Maj.-Gen. F. Graham CBE DSO, Colonel of the Regiment; Pipe Major R. Hill; Pipe Major A.Yule; the Pipe Major of the Argyll & Sutherland Highlanders of Canada; Pipe Major J. Weatherstone MBE BEM.

seven

The steady slog 1969–2004

Above: On return from Aden, the 1st Battalion was greeted by the news that, in company with several other regiments, it was to be disbanded. A vigorous campaign to 'Save the Argylls' attracted enormous public support and over a million signatures. This shook the Labour Government sufficiently to make it change to reducing the Argylls and others to a token company apiece.

Left: The Argyll Company was given the name 'Balaklava' Company and was posted to Gibraltar under the command of Maj. (later Brigadier) Iain Purves-Hume. Her Majesty gave her full support to the regiment and came to Stirling to inspect the company before its departure. She is here seen inspecting the ranks accompanied by the Company Commander and the CO of the 1st Battalion, Lt-Col. (later Lt-Gen. Sir) Sandy Boswell.

'Balaklava' Company, to whom the colours of the 1st Battalion had been entrusted, march past Her Majesty the Queen on a damp Stirling Castle esplanade. Battalion personnel not selected to serve in the company were posted to other units, the majority to other Scottish regiments.

After a successful tour in Gibraltar, the return of a Conservative Government saw the restoration of 'Balaklava' Company to full battalion strength. The 1st Battalion reformed at Kirknewton where, on 17 January 1973, 'Balaklava' Company symbolically handed back the colours to the resurrected Battalion. From left to right: Lt-Col. Patrick Palmer, CO of the Battalion; Maj.-Gen. Freddy Graham CBE DSO, Colonel of the Regiment and Maj. Iain Purves-Hume, OC 'Balaklava' Company.

Later that year, the Queen presented new colours to the 1st Battalion at a splendid parade held in the King's Park, Edinburgh. Here, she hands over the Queen's Colour, handed to her by Maj. Alastair Scott-Elliot, to Lt K.P.A. Barclay, while 2nd-Lt D.N. MacGregor-Smith awaits the Regimental Colour, held by Maj. Rod Stewart Lyddon.

After the Presentation, the Queen dined with her officers in the Mess at Kirknewton. She was escorted into the Mess by the CO, Lt-Col. Patrick Palmer (later Gen. Sir Patrick Palmer KBE KCVO, Governor of Windsor Castle). Her Majesty wears her Family Orders above the sash of The Order of the Thistle, on which is pinned the regimental brooch given to her by the regiment on her assumption of the Colonelcy in 1947.

Above: In 1974, the former Borough of Tarbert wished to confer an honour on the regiment. No longer able to confer its freedom, the 12th Duke of Argyll, a former Regular Officer of the Regiment, as Keeper of the Royal Castle of Tarbert, officially appointed the Colonel of the Regiment for the time being as Captain of the Castle, with a magnificent gold key bearing his arms as the mark of his office. The occasion was marked by a parade through the streets of the town.

Right: By 1976, the 1st Battalion was once more in Germany. Here, Drum Major Park displays exemplary smartness on parade at the head of the Massed Military Bands. His baldric as well as the Royal Cypher and Regimental Crest displays the regiment's Battle Honours while his single Campaign Service Medal shows no less than four campaign bars.

Left: For over thirty years, the 1st Battalion has spent much of its time in Northern Ireland, keeping the peace in a difficult, monotonous and dangerous role, which allowed no relaxation. Its staunchness and tenacity has earned it much praise; it has sustained a considerable number of casualties while performing an unglamorous but sadly vital task.

Below: As ever in an Internal Security situation, intelligence is vital. Here, in a cold and cramped observation post, dug in and heavily concealed, two members of the Battalion keep observation on a suspect location. Such tasks could last for days on end.

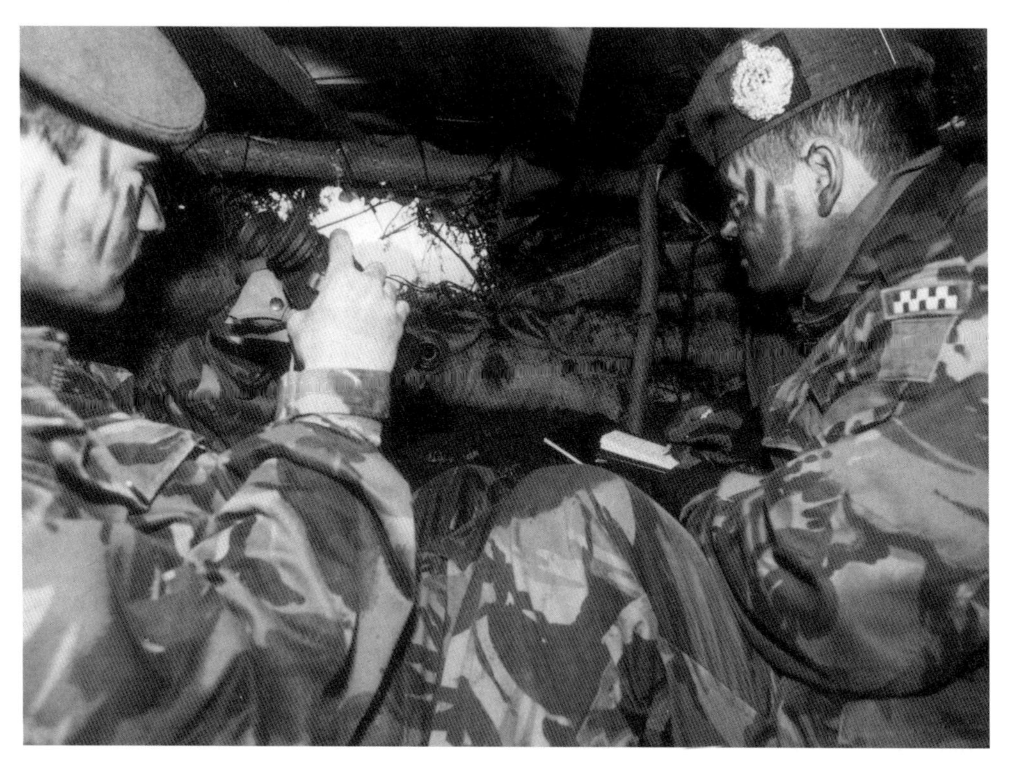

By contrast to the former photograph, controlling a riot could be all too eventful with stones, bricks, firebombs and bullets all possible hazards. Here, men of the 1st Battalion form up, shields and batons at the ready, their respirators on their heads, prepared to deal with a riot in Dungiven in 1971.

Helicopters are now so much a part of the scene as to be unworthy of comment. They played a major part in Northern Ireland where road travel was frequently hazardous, providing a speedy means of transport and insertion. Here, a patrol embarks on a Lynx helicopter, carrying their Bergen rucksacks with several days' supplies.

A dismounted vehicle patrol keeps a sharp lookout; even the tranquil fields of Ulster hide nasty surprises. The vehicle is strengthened by light armour and wire mesh over its more vulnerable parts.

All-round defence as this patrol makes its careful way through a back garden. The contrast between familiar peaceful domestic surroundings and the constant threat of attack made life all the more stressful.

The security situation is sufficiently relaxed to permit the wearing of the red and white diced regimental glengarry – less threatening than the camouflaged steel helmet – yet this Argyll keeps an ever-watchful eye over the streets of Belfast in 1973.

Two small boys enjoy the crack; alas, next day they will probably be throwing stones.

Back to civilisation, this time based in Colchester, the Recce Platoon on exercise in their skilfully camouflaged Fox fighting vehicle with its 30mm Rarden cannon.

Her Majesty and the Minister of Defence. The Rt Hon. George Younger MP served as a Major in the 7th Battalion, having fought in Korea as a National Service Officer of the 1st Battalion. He commanded the detachment of the Queen's Body Guard for Scotland on parade at the presentation of colours to the 3rd Battalion, 51st Highland Volunteers (Argyll & Sutherland Highlanders) at Stirling in July 1986. Also with Her Majesty are, on the left, the Colonel of the Regiment, the future Gen. Sir Patrick Palmer, and his predecessor, Lt-Gen. Sir Alexander Boswell KBE, Colonel Commandant of the Scottish Division.

Right: In November 1986, the 1st Battalion were sent to garrison the Falkland Islands and ensure there was no repetition of the ill-judged Argentinian intervention a few years previously. Here, Privates Baillie 54, Morris, Reid 39 and Gilmour patrol the perimeter of Stanley airfield.

Below: On exercise in rugged terrain; 2nd-Lt Sutherland gives out his orders as his men prepare to move out after a beach-landing on West Falkland. Behind, an unfamiliar but highly useful BV 206 all-terrain vehicle. The tour of duty in the South Atlantic came to an end in March 1987.

Above: In 1993 and 1999 (shown here) the 1st Battalion sent a platoon on active service to Bosnia; on this occasion their task was to boost the strength of 1st Battalion, The Royal Highland Fusiliers.

Left: Home-based tours of duty were interspersed with training overseas; in 2000, for instance, the 1st Battalion went to Kenya; here, Pte Macleod is seen with three Samburu tribesmen from Dol Dol.

Above: As a complete contrast to active service and overseas training exercises, the 1st Battalion has performed its share of ceremony; in 1988 it took over Public Duties from the Foot Guards in London; here, the Guard under Maj. A.K. Miller is formed up in the forecourt of Buckingham Palace.

Right: In 1996 the Queen presented new colours to replace those presented in 1973. The parade took place at Redford Barracks where the Battalion was now stationed. The old colours are trooped in front of the Battalion for the last time.

Left: The old colours are laid up for safe-keeping in the Regimental Museum, Stirling Castle; the Colonel of the Regiment, Maj.-Gen. David Thomson CB CBE MC, hands over the Regimental Colour. Gen. Thomson, who had won the Military Cross in Borneo, served in Aden as Col. Colin Mitchell's Adjutant. His final posting before retiring was as Senior Army Member of the Directing Staff of the Royal College of Defence Studies.

Below: Men of the 1st Battalion guard the Scottish Crown as it is taken under escort from Edinburgh Castle to the opening of the new Scottish Parliament by Her Majesty the Queen.

eight

Iraq 2004

In January 2004 the 1st Battalion embarked on a six-month tour of Iraq; their task not only to keep order over a vast area of southern Iraq but to train up a Brigade of the new Iraqi Army – the Iraq Civil Defence Corps – and the police. Both tasks were carried out in exemplary fashion with the new Brigade parading in June to mark the transition of authority to the Iraqi people. Here, the parade marches on, led by the Pipes and Drums.

A vehicle patrol through Safwan; all ranks on the alert. The teeming streets could so easily produce a grenade, a suicide bomb or a howling mob. Many of the population carried arms as a matter of course and were all too keen to use them. Bases were sniped, bombed and mortared regularly.

Another patrol on the lookout; trouble could and did come from any direction at any time. There were a host of incidents and the Battalion sustained several casualties but gave considerably more than it got.

Muster Parade and Maj. A.W.A. Griffiths, OC 'B' Company, surveys Iraqi recruits. While Argyll companies trained Iraqi battalions and Argyll platoons trained Iraqi companies, the individual Jock and Junior NCO found himself in charge of a section; in spite of language difficulties an enormous amount was achieved. Indeed, 'B' Company were tasked with raising and training a second battalion.

Maj. N.A. P. Wright, OC 'A' Company, congratulates a successful recruit on his promotion; initially supervised by the Argylls on operations, by the end of six months, units of the ICDC were operating to keep the peace under their own command. Both Maj. Wright and Maj. Griffith were decorated for gallantry during the campaign in Iraq.

A Landrover patrol approaches one of Saddam Hussein's triumphal arches, under observation from a sangar on the roof of the building on the far side of the road. Insurgents regularly attacked such patrols with Rocket Propelled Grenades and small-arms fire; they met with a warm reply and suffered many casualties.

While the cat's away … The officers' wives surprise their husbands with a poster specially composed to show what was happening back at home. Gen. Freddy Graham is not sure whether he approves.

The Pipes and Drums play in the grotesque splendour of one of Saddam's palaces.

Members of the Pipes and Drums try out Saddam s throne for size.

If vehicle maintenance is not your strong point, the old ways are best. Members of the MT (Moke Transport) Section!

The picture that needs no caption! The parade is dismissed and the families are reunited. Welcome home!

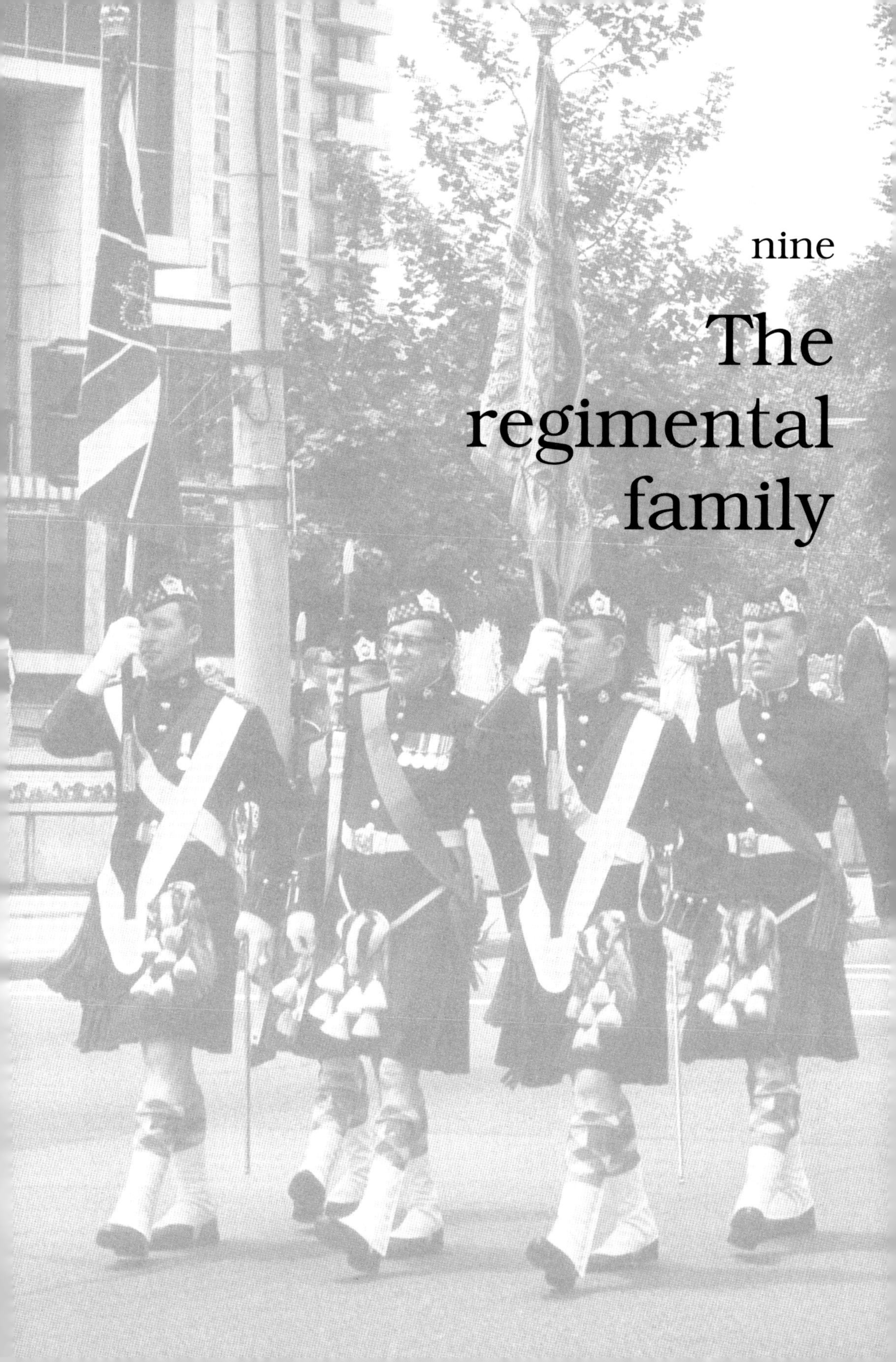

nine

The regimental family

As well as its own members, Regulars, Volunteers and Cadets, the regimental family includes affiliations with the Argyll & Sutherland Highlanders of Canada; the Calgary Highlanders; The Royal New South Wales Regiment; The 1st Battalion, The Frontier Force Regiment, Pakistan Army and HMS *Argyll* together with a fraternal link with the Royal Marines. Here, the Pipe Major of the Argyll & Sutherland Highlanders of Canada plays on the ramparts of Stirling Castle. Raised as the 91st Canadian Highlanders in 1903, the regiment adopted its present title in 1920. The picture above was taken during one of the Canadian Argylls' several appearances at the Edinburgh Military Tattoo.

The Colour Party of the Argyll & Sutherland Highlanders on parade. The Canadians wear the uniform of the 'Imperial' Regiment with minor variations and march past to 'The Campbells are Coming'. The colours bear honours for the First World War, in which they raised two battalions of the Canadian Expeditionary Force as well as providing a company for the 16th Battalion, The Canadian Scottish. In the Second World War, one of their battalions garrisoned Jamaica before proceeding overseas as part of the 4th Canadian Armoured Division fighting from Normandy to the Baltic.

In 1938 the regiment formed an alliance with the Australian 41st Byron Regiment. When re-raised in 1948, this unit became the 41st Infantry Battalion, The Byron Scottish and adopted a uniform based on that of the Argylls. Now the 41st Battalion Royal New South Wales Regiment, the unit still wears the kilt on ceremonial occasions. This 1956 group features 'B' Company of The Byron Scottish.

The regiment is affiliated to HMS *Argyll*, a Type 23 Duke Class frigate named after the Duke of Argyll. A strong link is maintained with the ship, which has regularly taken parties of Jocks to sea.

Above: Quarter Guard of the 1st Battalion, The Frontier Force Regiment, Pakistan Army. The regiment's link to the Argylls goes back to the Second World War when, as the 6th Royal Battalion (Scinde) 13th Frontier Force Rifles, they fought alongside the 91st in Italy, notably at the defence of Monte Cerere in December 1944 when, together, they beat off a heavy attack by the German 1st Parachute Division.

Left: The immaculate Provost Sergeant outside the Barracks Gate. The Rifles presented the 1st Battalion with a silver statuette of their Havildar Tara Singh and his Vickers Machine Gun to commemorate the battle. It was highly valued and when the original was sadly lost in a fire in the Officers' Mess in Northern Ireland, considerable trouble was taken to have a replacement made.

The Calgary Highlanders were raised in 1910 as the 103rd Regiment (Calgary Rifles). In 1921 the 1st Battalion became a Highland regiment as the Calgary Highlanders and in 1925 was formally affiliated to the Argyll & Sutherland Highlanders. Her Majesty is Colonel-in-Chief of the Regiment and is here seen seated with the officers. Note the Sikh officer in the turban.

As Colonel of the Argylls, Gen. Sir Patrick Palmer inspects the Calgary Highlanders. Sticklers for correct turnout will note that he is wearing the red tabs of a General Officer rather than the correct regimental collar badges!

Warrant Officer Bruce Waterhouse, CD The Calgary Highlanders, formerly a Corporal of the 1st Battalion, Argyll & Sutherland Highlanders. The late Bruce Waterhouse came from Calgary to serve with the 1st Battalion before returning to his parent regiment in Canada.

Rather too much make-up? A cheerful and still photogenic member of the 7th/8th Battalion Argyll & Sutherland Highlanders TA on exercise. Women now play a full role as part of the TA which itself is now an increasingly vital provider of manpower for the operations in which the Regular Army is involved.

Above: The role of the Cadets has never been more important, both as producing good citizens and potential recruits for the Regular and the Reserve Forces. With the reduction in the Army's numbers, the regiment depends more and more on the Army Cadet Force to impose the regimental footprint on the regimental area. A group of the Argyll & Sutherland Highlanders Cadet Battalion pose for the camera.

Right: One thing, however, is sure. The Argylls, in whatever guise, will continue to soldier on, facing whatever comes their way with courage, invincible cheerfulness and determination and mindful of their great heritage.

Other titles published by Tempus

Moon Over Malaya: A Tale of Argylls and Marines

JONATHAN MOFFATT & AUDREY HOLMES MCCORMICK

Britain's worst military disaster is looked at here in a new light using first-hand accounts from the men on the ground. Their story is told for the first time and is conclusive proof that some of our soldiers did fight the enemy and, in fact, held them back for long enough to enable many to escape to Singapore to fight again. For some, escape was no option and they ended up in Japanese PoW camps, where they suffered greatly.

07524 2690 7

The Black Watch

THE BLACK WATCH PHOTOGRAPHIC ARCHIVE

This is a stirring history of one of Britain's finest regiments since its first images were recorded some 150 years ago. Over 200 photographs have been selected to represent different aspects of regimental life, both at home and abroad, in peace and war. *The Black Watch* contains photographs of heroes as well as other famous people, most notably HM Queen Elizabeth the Queen Mother'.

07524 1763 0

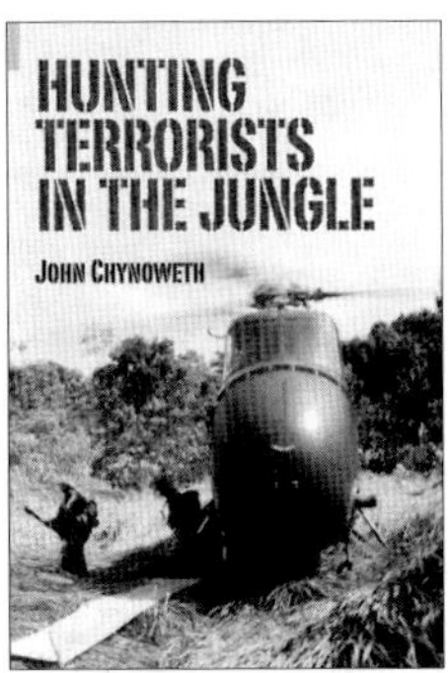

Hunting Terrorists in the Jungle

JOHN CHYNOWETH

This is the dramatic story of one young lieutenant who had been transported from his home in England and trained to kill Chinese Communist terrorists in Malaya. John Chynoweth spent most of 1953 and 1954 as a platoon commander in the Malay Regiment. As the story of the Malayan Emergency from the soldier's viewpoint, this fascinating take should be of interest to ex-National Servicemen everywhere.

07524 3419 5

The Scots Guards

WILLIAM F. HENDRIE & JACK SMITH

The troops of the Scots Guards have served Britain for three centuries, which is a record few can match. This book contains over 200 pictures of the regiment and its men at their best, in battle and in play, and the images and accompanying text are a unique record of a unique regiment.

07524 2399 1